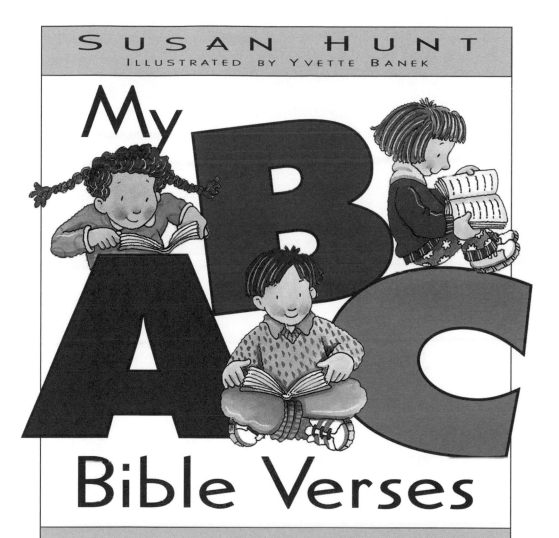

SUSAN HUNT

ILLUSTRATED BY YVETTE BANEK

My ABC

Bible Verses

Hiding God's Word in Little Hearts

 **CROSSWAY**

WHEATON, ILLINOIS

Dedicated to the memory of our seventh grandchild
Annie Grace Barriault

Before her birth our family prayer was that Annie Grace's life
would be a celebration of God's glorious grace and that she would
always rest in the sufficiency of His grace.

In eleven brief weeks she accomplished that mission.
Because God entrusted Annie Grace to our family,
we know Him better, and we love Him more.

Through her life and death, the body of Christ demonstrated
the reality of grace as they enfolded us in love.

This covenant child is safe in the arms of Jesus.
My prayer is that this book will be used to guide other little ones
to know the wonder of His amazing grace.

♥

My ABC Bible Verses

Copyright © 1998 by Susan Hunt

Published by Crossway, 1300 Crescent Street, Wheaton, Illinois 60187

Design: Cindy Kiple

Printed in Singapore

Unless otherwise designated, Scripture references are taken from the *New King James Version*.
Copyright © 1982, Thomas Nelson, Inc. Used by permission.

Scripture references designated KJV are taken from the King James Version of the Bible.

The author may be contacted at PCA Christian Education and Publications,
1700 N. Brown Road, Lawrenceville, GA 30043. Phone: 678-825-1100.

THIS MATERIAL IS ALSO AVAILABLE IN CURRICULUM FORMAT. CALL 800-283-1357.

Library of Congress Cataloging-in-Publication Data
Hunt, Susan, 1940-
    My ABC Bible verses : hiding God's Word in little hearts / Susan Hunt.
      p. cm.
    ISBN 13: 978-1-58134-005-1 (alk. paper)
    ISBN 10: 1-58134-005-2
    1. Bible—Memorizing.   2. Alphabet rhymes.   3. Christian education—
      Home training.   I. Title.
BS617.7.H86   1998
220.5'2036—dc21   98-17102

Crossway is a publishing ministry of Good News Publishers.

IM		17	16	15	14	13	12
23	22	21	20	19	18	17	16

Dear lover of children,

The psalmist said, "Thy word have I hid in mine heart, that I might not sin against thee" (Psalm 119:11 KJV). God's Word fortifies our children against sin because it tells them about Jesus and their need for Him. The person who helps a child hide the Word in his or her heart gives that child a rich inheritance. Many testify that they have never forgotten the verses they memorized as children. Many also testify that they have never forgotten the person who taught them the Word. This book is written to help you give a precious legacy to the children you love. The stories in it are designed for you to read aloud to them.

The Scripture verses are from the New King James Version *or the* King James Version *of the Bible. There is a beauty, dignity, and a cadence about the King James Version that I believe is beneficial for memorization.*

God's Word is the infallible, authoritative rule for faith and practice. Most of the verses in this book are about how we practice what we believe, but our practice must never be separated from what we believe. I have written these stories to teach children about grace. We must never hold God's Word before our children as a standard of behavior that they can achieve in their own effort. These stories remind the child about his or her need for the Holy Spirit to give grace to obey. We are saved by grace, and we live by grace. We must not teach our children anything less than the splendor and the sufficiency of God's grace.

For His glory,

Susan Hunt

Dear little friend,

The Bible is God's Word. It is His love letter to His people. In the Bible God tells us what He wants us to know and what He wants us to do.

Psalm 119:11 says, "Your word I have hidden in my heart, that I might not sin against You."

To hide God's Word in our hearts means to memorize it. When we hide God's Word in our hearts, we have a priceless treasure that no one can ever take away from us. We have a treasure that will help us know, love, and obey the holy and majestic God of heaven and earth.

God gives us another gift. He gives us His Holy Spirit to help us understand and obey His Word. As you memorize Bible verses, always remember to ask the Holy Spirit to help you understand and obey the verses you hide in your heart.

I pray that this book will help you hide God's Word in your heart, and I pray that His Spirit will give you grace to obey God's Word.

For God's glory,

"Miss" Susan

A soft answer turns away wrath.

PROVERBS 15:1

■ ♥ ■

The Bible is not just a book that some people wrote. It is the Word of God. The Bible is a precious gift from God to His children. When we hide it in our hearts, it will help us keep from sinning against God.

Proverbs 15:1 tells us that a soft answer turns away wrath. A soft answer is a kind and gentle answer. Wrath means anger.

This verse from God's Word teaches us that when someone is mean or unkind to us, we should respond by giving a kind answer. A gentle answer will turn away, or stop, an argument. ♥

Missy memorized Proverbs 15:1. Every day she prayed that God would help her to give soft answers if someone was unkind to her.

Missy and her friend Janet were playing with Missy's dolls. Janet said, "Let's put the dolls in the bathtub and give them a bath."

Missy said, "Oh no, Mom told me never to put these dolls in water."

Janet became angry. "Missy," she said, "I'm going home if you won't give the dolls a bath! I'm not going to be your friend anymore!"

Before Missy learned Proverbs 15:1, she would have said, "Well, you just go home. I don't want to be your friend either." But Missy remembered, *"A soft answer turns away wrath."* Then she said to

Janet, "I'm sorry. I want you to be my friend, but I can't disobey my mom."

Janet was angrily stomping out the door, but when she heard Missy speak so sweetly, she turned around and smiled. "Oh, Missy, I'm sorry. You're my best friend. It was wrong for me to ask you to disobey your mom."

The Holy Spirit helped Missy remember and obey God's Word that was hidden in her heart. Missy obeyed God and gave a kind answer to her friend, and it stopped the argument.

Something even more wonderful happened. God was glorified when Missy obeyed His Word.

LET'S TALK
When her friend was unkind, who helped Missy remember that "a soft answer turns away wrath"?

Who helped Missy give a kind answer?

Hide Proverbs 15:1 in *your* heart. Say it three times.

LET'S PRAY
Ask God to help you remember and obey this verse from His Word, even when someone is unkind to you.

Blessed are the peacemakers, for they shall be called sons of God.

MATTHEW 5:9

■ ♥ ■

When we are peacemakers, we show that we are God's children. We are all sinners. When we believe that Jesus died on the cross for our sins, God forgives us. Then we have peace with Him. We become members of His family. We are His children, and He is our heavenly Father. He gives us His power to be peacemakers. ♥

Missy hid Matthew 5:9 in her heart, and the Holy Spirit helped her to be a peacemaker. One rainy afternoon Missy and her brother Bill were playing with their toy cars and trucks. There was one little dump truck that Bill got for his birthday that they both loved to play with. When Missy picked it up, Bill grabbed it from her and said, "No, that's mine, and you can't play with it. I'm going to play with it."

Missy was so frustrated. Some harsh words were ready to jump out of her mouth. She started to say, "You are just mean and selfish! You don't know how to share."

Then something very wonderful happened. Missy remembered Matthew 5:9: *"Blessed are the peacemakers, for they shall be called sons of God."*

Missy did not want to be a troublemaker. She wanted to be

a peacemaker. "You're right, Bill," Missy said. "It's yours, and I should have asked you first. I'll play with something else."

Bill looked ashamed. He felt awful and was quite sorry. "I'm sorry, Missy. I was being a troublemaker, but you decided to be a peacemaker. Here, you can play with the dump truck."

Their mom walked into the room and gave Missy and Bill a great big hug. "I heard you being a peacemaker, Missy, and I'm very thankful. Bill, I'm also thankful that the Holy Spirit helped you realize that you were wrong. He gave you the grace to tell Missy that you were sorry. This shows me that you both love the Lord Jesus."

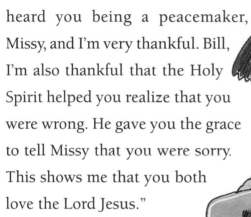

LET'S TALK

Who helped Missy to be a peacemaker?

Who helped Bill to be sorry for his sin?

Say Matthew 5:9 three times.

Say the A and B verses.

LET'S PRAY

Thank God that Jesus died on the cross for your sins so you can have peace with God. Ask God to help you to be a peacemaker.

Children, obey your parents in all things, for this is well pleasing to the Lord.

COLOSSIANS 3:20

■ ♥ ■

Colossians 3:20 tells us that children are to obey their parents. You don't obey your parents because they are bigger than you, but because God has put them in authority over you. When you obey your parents, you obey God, and this pleases Him. ♥

On Saturday mornings Missy and Bill know they are to clean their rooms before they play. They are to straighten their bookshelves, dust *thoroughly*, empty their trash cans, and take the sheets off their beds and put them in the laundry room.

One Saturday morning Missy and Bill were in a hurry to go outside because the kids in the neighborhood were planning a circus. Everyone was very excited. While Missy and Bill ate breakfast, they talked about the circus. They had taught their dog Mollie some tricks, and they could hardly wait for her to perform. Their dad reminded them about their Saturday morning chores. "Oh, Dad," they begged, "can we clean our rooms later?"

"No," said their dad. "I know this is a big day, but you must do your chores first."

Missy and Bill quickly finished breakfast and asked to be

excused. As they walked to their rooms, Missy whispered, "We have to hurry, Bill. Don't take time to dust the books, and don't take the things off your desk when you dust. Just hurry!"

In about five minutes they were running out the door. Soon they were with their friends, but they weren't having fun. They kept thinking about Colossians 3:20.

Finally Missy said, "Bill we disobeyed Mom and Dad this morning. We didn't please God in the way we cleaned our rooms."

"I know," said Bill. "Come on, let's go home and do it right this time."

When they got home, they hugged their mom. "We're sorry," they both said at the same time.

"Sorry for what?" she asked. Then they told her what they had done.

"I'm thankful that God helped you understand what it means to obey your parents, and that you want to please Him in everything you do. Now clean your rooms so you can get ready for the circus. We're sure you'll be the stars of the show!"

LET'S TALK
Why are children to obey their parents?
Say Colossians 3:20 three times.
Say the A, B, and C verses.
LET'S PRAY
Ask God to help you please Him by obeying your parents. Ask God to give your parents wisdom to teach you His Word.

Do all things without complaining and disputing.

PHILIPPIANS 2:14

■ ♥ ■

Sometimes we hear people whine and argue when they don't get their way. "I want ice cream! Why won't you buy me some ice cream?"

Sometimes people complain when they don't like something. "Why are we having beans for dinner? I hate beans!"

Philippians 2:14 says to "do all things without complaining and disputing." This means that God wants us to do everything without whining and arguing. ♥

Missy was sitting at the kitchen table putting her favorite puzzle together while her mother prepared dinner. "Missy," said her mother, "I need you to empty the trash."

Missy frowned. "Oh, Mom," she whined, "why do I have to empty the trash? Let Bill do it."

Missy's mom wiped her hands, picked up her Bible, and sat down beside Missy. She opened her Bible to Philippians 2:14 and read, "Do all things without complaining and disputing." Then she explained that God does not want us to whine and argue. God wants us to do everything with a kind, helpful, and thankful spirit.

"Missy," said her mom, "I understand why you whined

and complained, because many times I don't want to do *my* chores. I sometimes argue and complain about things I don't like. But that is wrong. We must ask the Holy Spirit to give us grace to be thankful in our hearts so we will be kind in our behavior. Let's pray that God will give you a thankful heart."

Missy thanked God for her mom, for her home, and even for the trash can that needed to be emptied. Then she thanked God for her arms and legs so she *could* empty the trash. After she said, "amen," Missy was actually excited about emptying the trash. Rather than whining and complaining, she said, "Wow, Mom. It's really cool that I can empty the trash. Thanks for letting me help you!"

At bedtime Missy told her Mom how thankful she was to have learned something new from God's Word. "I'm glad God gave us the Bible so that we can learn about Him and hear about Jesus who died for our sins. I'm glad He lets us know how He wants us to live and gives us the Holy Spirit to help us do the right things," Missy said as she nodded off to sleep.

LET'S TALK
What does complaining and disputing mean?

How can we have a thankful heart rather than a complaining heart?

Say Philippians 2:14 three times.

Say the verses for A, B, C, and D.

LET'S PRAY
Ask God for grace to have a thankful heart.

Even a child is known by his deeds.

PROVERBS 20:11

■ ♥ ■

People can tell what kind of child you are by the way you act. When people see the love of Jesus in you, they want to know about our Savior. ♥

Missy and Bill were grocery shopping with their mother. As they passed the candy aisle, Missy asked, "Mom, may we buy some candy?"

Her mom said, "Not today, Missy. We'll get some apples instead."

Missy almost complained and disputed, but she thought about Philippians 2:14. Then she said, "That's great, Mom. I love apples."

Another mom and her little girl were also grocery shopping. The little girl grabbed a box of candy and said, "I want this!"

Her mother said, "No, we can't buy that today." The little girl went into a frenzy. She cried and said unkind things to her mother and caused quite a disturbance.

When Missy, Bill, and their mom got to the checkout counter, Bill asked for money for the gum machine. His mom reminded him that the dentist had explained that gum was not good for his teeth. Bill did not argue.

The other woman and her little girl were behind Missy and Bill's mom. The little girl frowned at her mom and said, "Give me some money for the gum machine." The mother gave her some money. The little girl did not thank her mother.

While Missy and Bill's mom paid for the groceries, Mr. Richards, the store manager, walked over and said, "I've watched you since you came into the store. You have such good manners. You're so respectful. I can tell that you're nice children by the way you act."

Missy and Bill thanked him. Bill said, "Would you like to know why we act this way?"

"I sure would!" said Mr. Richards.

"It's because we love Jesus, and we want to obey Him. He helps us to act the way He wants us to act."

Missy and Bill's mom told Mr. Richards about their church and invited him to visit. The next Sunday Mr. Richards and his family were at church. They came every Sunday, and soon they all believed in Jesus.

LET'S TALK
Did Missy and Bill act the way they did because they were better than the other little girl?

Say Proverbs 20:11 three times.

Say the verses for A through E.

LET'S PRAY
Ask Jesus for grace to act the way He wants you to act so that He will be glorified and so that people will know that you belong to Him.

For God so loved the world that He gave His only begotten Son, that whoever believes in Him should not perish but have everlasting life.

JOHN 3:16

■ ♥ ■

On the first Christmas God gave His Son Jesus to us. Jesus left heaven and came to earth so that we would not have to perish. To perish means to die. Of course, our bodies will die someday, but if we believe in Jesus, our souls will live forever with God. ♥

Christmas was just one week away. Missy and Bill memorized John 3:16 to say when their grandparents would come to visit. Each time Missy and Bill said John 3:16, they understood more about the meaning of Christmas, and they were more thankful for God's Christmas gift to them.

They were excited about celebrating Jesus' birthday. "Just think," said Missy, "God loves us so much that He gave Jesus as a gift to us so we can have everlasting life with Him in heaven."

"Wait a minute!" said Bill. "It is Jesus' birthday. Why don't we give a birthday gift to *Him?*"

"That's a great idea!" Missy exclaimed. "What can we give Him?"

They thought and thought. What *could* they give to the Lord Jesus?

At breakfast on Sunday morning their dad said, "Let's pray for your choir. You will be singing praises to Jesus today. Your songs of praise are a special gift to Him."

"That's cool!" said Missy. "We tried to think of a birthday present to give to Jesus. When we sing today, I'm going to think about my songs having a big bow on them and a card saying, 'Happy Birthday, Jesus.'"

After church Missy and Bill saw Mr. Benson picking up bulletins and putting hymnbooks in the pew racks.

"Can we help you, Mr. Benson?" asked Bill.

He smiled at them. "You're an answer to prayer! Your time is a special gift you can give to Jesus."

Missy and Bill looked at each other and grinned. "Do you mean that helping you is a gift to Jesus?" asked Missy.

"Wow!" exclaimed Bill. "Our songs of praise and our time are gifts we can give to Jesus. Thank you for letting us help you, Mr. Benson."

LET'S TALK

John 3:16 teaches us that God loves us so much that He gave us a special gift. What is that gift?

John 3:16 teaches us that if we believe in Jesus, we will have what?

What gift can you give to Jesus?

Say John 3:16 three times.

Say the verses for A through F.

LET'S PRAY

Thank God for giving His Son to die for our sins so we can live with Him forever.

Go into all the world and preach the gospel to every creature.

MARK 16:15

— ■ ♥ ■ —

In Mark 16:15 Jesus gives us a very important assignment. He tells us to go to all the world and preach the Gospel to every creature. Gospel means good news. The good news is: For God so loved the world that He gave His only begotten Son, that whoever believes in Him should not perish but have everlasting life (John 3:16).

People in Japan, Brazil, India, the United States, and everywhere in the world need to know that God loves His world so much that He sent His only Son so that we can have eternal life. God calls some people to go as missionaries to other countries to tell people about Jesus. But this verse is not just for missionaries. This verse is for us. We can tell people about Jesus right in our own neighborhood. ♥

A new family moved in across the street from Missy and Bill. Missy and Bill helped their mom make a cake for the new family. Then they prayed and asked the Lord to help them to be missionaries to their new neighbors.

The new family had a little girl Missy's age. Missy and Carol played together every day. Missy asked Carol if she would like to go to Sunday school. "I've never been to Sunday school, but I'll ask Mom if I can go."

Carol loved Sunday school. She went with Missy every Sunday. Missy's mom and dad invited Carol's mom and dad, but they were not interested in hearing about Jesus. Every day Missy and Bill and their parents prayed for Carol's family.

One day Carol's mother talked to Missy's mom. "We see a difference in Carol since she started going to church. She talks about Jesus and how much she loves Him. She's more loving and kind, and she says it's because the Holy Spirit helps her. Her dad and I want to go to church with you and learn more about Jesus."

On Sunday Carol's mom and dad listened very carefully to the pastor. They both asked Jesus to be their Savior. Later they thanked Missy for being a missionary to Carol, and they thanked Carol for being a missionary to them.

LET'S TALK

What is the Gospel?

Do children have to wait until they are adults to tell people the good news?

Say Mark 16:15 three times.

Say John 3:16.

LET'S PRAY

Ask God to help you to be a missionary and to tell people about Jesus. Pray for missionaries who are serving God in other countries.

Honor your father and your mother.

EXODUS 20:12

■ ♥ ■

To honor means to value, to appreciate, to love, and to respect. Sometimes children do what their parents tell them, but they have a bad attitude. That is not real obedience. Children should obey with a respectful and grateful attitude, and they can only do that by God's grace.

Asking God for grace to help you honor your parents even when they discipline you is really hard. In fact, it is impossible. But God gives us power to do what we cannot do in our own strength. ♥

Bill knows he is not allowed to go to his friend Jimmy's house alone because he has to cross a busy street to get there. One day Jimmy called and said, "Bill, I just got a new swing set. Come play with me." Bill told his mom he was going outside to play. Then he opened the gate to their fence and walked to Jimmy's house.

When Bill's mom looked outside and did not see him, she was frightened. She looked everywhere. The telephone rang. It was Jimmy's mom. "Did you know that Bill is here?" she asked.

Bill and Jimmy were playing on Jimmy's new swings. Bill's stomach felt yucky, and it was not because he was swinging so high. Bill knew he had lied to his mom, and he had disobeyed her. When he saw her car drive into Jimmy's yard, he began to cry. His mom swooped him up in her arms and hugged him. "Bill, I was so frightened."

"I'm sorry," Bill sobbed.

As they drove home, Bill's mom said, "Bill, you know that I have to punish you. I love you, and I must teach you to do what is right."

"That's okay," said Bill. "I'm glad that you love me and care about me. Thank you."

Bill had prayed that God would give him grace to honor his parents. God answered that prayer. The Holy Spirit helped Bill to be grateful and respectful even when he was going to be punished.

LET'S TALK

Is it always easy to honor our parents?

If a child does what his parents tell him, but he has a bad attitude, is that real obedience?

How can we have a heart that honors our parents?

Say Exodus 20:12 three times.

Say the C verse and the H verse.

LET'S PRAY

Ask God to give you grace to obey and honor your parents.

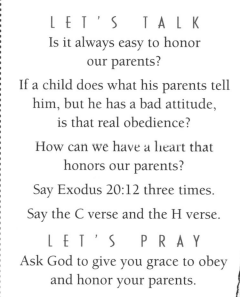

I can do all things through Christ who strengthens me.

PHILIPPIANS 4:13

• ♥ •

"All things" means all the things God tells us to do in the Bible. The strength that Jesus gives is spiritual strength and the grace we need to obey God's Word. ♥

One day Missy was quite upset. She was trying to learn to jump rope. She tried a few times and got all tangled up. Missy threw the jump rope down and grumbled. "I just can't do it! I'll never learn."

Missy's mother watched from the kitchen window. "Would you like a snack?" she asked. As she poured a glass of juice, she said, "Missy, I've noticed that you don't work at something until you learn it. Philippians 4:13 says: 'I can do all things through Christ who strengthens me.' This doesn't mean we can do everything perfectly—like jump rope. But it does mean we can do all the things God tells us to do in His Word. Missy, listen and tell me *how* we can do all the things Jesus wants us to do. Where do we get the strength?"

Missy listened as her mom repeated Philippians 4:13.

"Jesus strengthens us," said Missy. "He gives us muscles?"

Her mom laughed. "Well, Missy, it doesn't mean muscles in our bodies. It means that Jesus gives us *spiritual* strength in our hearts and minds. He gives us grace to obey God's Word. So I guess He gives us spiritual muscles."

Missy went back outside to practice jumping rope. Her friend Jennifer came over. Jennifer laughed at Missy. "You're so clumsy. I can jump rope better than you."

Missy almost said, "I can ride my bike without training wheels. You're a baby with those training wheels on your bike." Before the words came out, Missy remembered, *"A soft answer turns away wrath."* But she was so angry she thought, *I can't give Jennifer a soft answer. I'm too mad.* Then she remembered, *"I can do all things through Christ who strengthens me."* Missy whispered a prayer in her heart. *"Jesus, please give me spiritual muscles to give a soft answer to Jennifer."*

Jennifer was still laughing, but Missy didn't feel angry anymore. She laughed too. "I know I look funny," she said. "Will you help me learn how to jump rope?"

"Sure, Missy, and I'm sorry I laughed at you. If I help you learn how to jump rope, will you help me learn how to ride my bike?"

LET'S TALK

What does Jesus give us strength to do?

Say Philippians 4:13 three times.

The verses for A, B, C, D, E, G, and H tell us some of the things God tells us to do.
Say these verses.

LET'S PRAY

Thank God that Jesus died for our sins and that He gives us spiritual strength to obey His Word.

Jesus said to him, "I am the way, the truth, and the life. . . ."

J O H N   1 4 : 6

■ ♥ ■

In John 14:6 Jesus tells us three things about Himself. Listen carefully and see if you can tell what they are.

"Jesus said to him, 'I am the way, the truth, and the life.'" ♥

Missy and Bill's family were on a picnic. They took a walk through the woods. After they walked for a while, Bill said, "Where are we? How will we get back to our car?"

Bill's dad said, "Don't worry, Bill. I'll show you the way."

A little later Bill's dad reminded Bill and Missy about when Jesus said, "I am the way." "Jesus was telling us that He is the way to heaven," said their dad. "And there can be no sin in heaven. We are sinners, but Jesus died on the cross so that our sins can be forgiven. He is the way we can get to heaven."

"Besides that," said their mom, "Jesus also said that He is the truth. Everything we read in the Bible is true because it is God's Word, and God is truth."

While Bill and his family were on the picnic, they met another family. The children had fun playing together while the adults talked. On the way home Bill's dad said, "We need to pray for our new friends. They aren't Christians. They don't believe in Jesus, and they don't believe that the Bible is true."

Missy and Bill were amazed. "I thought everyone believes the Bible is true," said Bill.

"No, Bill," explained his dad. "Many people don't believe there is such a thing as absolute truth. But we must remember that the only reason we believe is because of God's grace. We must pray for those who don't know that Jesus is the way, the truth, and the life. We must pray that they will believe in Jesus so they will have life."

"But don't we already have life?" asked Bill.

"Yes, Bill," said his dad. "Your body is alive. That's physical life. But Jesus came to give you spiritual life. That means He gives you eternal life in your soul so that you will live with Him forever in heaven. So what have you two learned today?"

"That Jesus is the way to heaven because He died on the cross for our sins," answered Bill. "And that He is the truth, and everything He tells us is true."

"Jesus is the life too," chimed in Missy, "and He gives us eternal life."

"That's right, kids," smiled their dad. "Jesus is a wonderful Savior and is everything we need."

L E T ' S   T A L K

What three things does Jesus tell us about Himself in John 14:6?

Say John 14:6 three times.

Say the verses for A through E.

L E T ' S   P R A Y

Thank God that Jesus is the way, the truth, and the life.

Keep your tongue from evil.

PSALM 34:13

■ ♥ ■

God wants us to hide His Word in our hearts so that we will not sin against Him. When we memorize God's Word, the Holy Spirit teaches us what God wants us to know and how He wants us to behave. The Holy Spirit helps us obey God's Word.

Psalm 34:13 tells us to keep our tongue from evil. We surely do need for God to give us grace to obey this command. ♥

There was a new girl in Missy's kindergarten class. When the teacher introduced Sally, Missy's friend Marie whispered, "I don't think I like her. Let's not play with her."

On the way home from school, Missy's mom said, "Tell me about your day."

"A new girl came to our class today, but Marie and I don't like her."

"I have a new Bible verse for you, Missy," said her mom. "Psalm 34 says, 'Keep your tongue from evil.' What do you think this means?"

"I guess God is telling us not to say mean, unkind things," said Missy. "Mom, I said unkind things about Sally. What should I do?"

"Missy, I'm thankful that the Holy Spirit made your heart tender so that you realize you disobeyed God's Word. I'm also thankful that God gave you grace to be sorry that you disobeyed Him. First, you should ask God to forgive you. Then you should ask Him for *wisdom* to know what you should do and for *grace* to obey Him.

Missy, it's impossible for us to keep our tongues from evil in our own strength. Every day we need to ask God to give us grace to use our tongues for His glory."

The next day when Missy and Marie walked into the classroom, Sally was standing alone looking at a book. Marie said, "I don't like her."

"Marie," said Missy, "I learned a new Bible verse yesterday that says, 'Keep your tongue from evil.' It's wrong for us to say bad things about someone. God wants us to use our tongues to say kind things. Sally looks lonely. I think we should ask her to play with us."

Missy was nervous because she didn't know if Marie would be angry with her, but Marie smiled and said, "You're right, Missy. Let's go talk to Sally."

Soon the three girls were having fun putting a puzzle together.

LET'S TALK

Can we keep our tongue from saying evil things in our own strength?

Sometimes we are not sure how to use our tongue for God's glory. What should we ask God to give us so that we will know what to say?

Psalm 34:13 has five words. Say it five times.

Say the verses for F through K.

LET'S PRAY

Ask God for grace to keep your tongue from evil and for wisdom to know what you should say that will glorify Him.

Let your light so shine before men, that they may see your good works and glorify your Father in heaven.

MATTHEW 5:16

■ ♥ ■

Sometimes it takes courage to let our light shine, but God will give us strength to do what He tells us to do. Then others will see our good works and glorify our Father in heaven. ♥

Before dinner Missy and Bill's dad reads a verse from God's Word, someone thanks God for the food, and then the family talks about the verse during dinner. One night their dad read Matthew 5:16.

Bill had an inquisitive look on his face. "Does this mean we should have a flashlight so people can see our good works?"

Bill's dad smiled. "Not quite. The light is the light of God's truth. The Bible talks about sin as darkness and truth as light. The Holy Spirit shines the light of God's truth into our hearts. Then, when we obey God's Word, we shine that light out so others can see it. When you give a soft answer, or when you are a peacemaker, or when you keep your tongue from evil, the light of God's truth shines through you."

Now Missy had a puzzled look on her face. "But if they see *our* good works, why will they glorify *God?*" she asked.

"God is glorified because He gives us power to know and to do His truth," explained their dad. "Remember when Mr. Richards saw you in the supermarket? When he said you were nice children, you told him that you act the way you do because you love Jesus. Mr. Richards saw your good works, but when he understood that your behavior is a result of God's grace, He glorified God. He attended our church and heard the Gospel. He trusted Jesus to be his Savior. Now his light shines for Jesus."

The next day on the playground at school, Tommy shoved Bill. He tried to get Bill to fight. Tommy said, "What's the matter? Are you afraid?"

Suddenly Bill was so angry that he almost hit Tommy. Then he remembered Matthew 5:16. Bill wanted to let his light shine so that Tommy would glorify God. "No, I'm not afraid," said Bill, "but Jesus doesn't want us to fight."

Their teacher came over to see what was wrong. Tommy was very honest. "I tried to get Bill to fight, but he wouldn't because he wants to obey Jesus. I was wrong, and I'm sorry."

"Bill, that was a very brave thing for you to do," said the teacher.

LET'S TALK
Why will God be glorified when others see our good works?

Is it always easy to let our light shine for Jesus?

Say Matthew 5:16 three times.

Say the verses for A through C.

LET'S PRAY
Ask God to shine the light of His truth into your heart, and ask Him to give you grace to obey His truth so that His light will shine out to others.

My little children, let us not love in word or in tongue, but in deed and in truth.

1 JOHN 3:18

■ ♥ ■

To love in deed means that we show our love by the things we do.

To love in truth means that we show our love the way God tells us to in His Word. ♥

Missy and Bill's bedtime routine is the same every night. Their family sits on the floor and reads a story, they pray, everyone gets hugs and kisses, and then Missy and Bill go to their rooms and get in their beds. Then Missy calls, "I love you" to Bill, and he calls, "I love you too" to Missy.

One day it was cold and rainy so Missy and Bill could not go outside to play. By afternoon they were bored and grumpy. Bill was irritated with Missy because she was playing a computer game and would not let him play with her. Later Missy was annoyed with Bill because he would not share his Legos with her. At dinner Bill said to his dad, "Missy was selfish today. She wouldn't let me play with her."

Missy quickly responded, "Well, Bill was selfish too. He wouldn't share his Legos with me." They both were angry with the other for tattling.

After dinner they went through their regular bedtime routine, even the part where Missy called, "I love you, Bill," and Bill said, "I love you too, Missy." But this night something different happened. Their dad walked into Bill's room and said, "Get on my back, Bill. I'm taking you for a ride."

They went to Missy's room. "I have a Bible verse for you," said their dad. He read 1 John 3:18. "You said the words, 'I love you' to each other, but you haven't loved each other in deed and in truth. You've been angry and unkind to each other. I know that it's hard to love in deed and in truth. In fact, it's impossible in our own strength. When we begin to feel annoyed with someone, we must quickly ask God to give us grace to love in deed and in truth."

"Dad," said Missy, "I really do love Bill, but sometimes he makes me angry. I'm glad we have the Holy Spirit to help us love each other."

"Me too," said Bill.

LET'S TALK
What does it mean to love in deed and in truth?

Does Jesus just say that He loves us? What did He do to show His love to us?

Say 1 John 3:18 three times.

Say the verses for D through F.

LET'S PRAY
Ask God to give you grace to love others in deed and in truth.

No one can serve two masters.

MATTHEW 6:24

■ ♥ ■

God tells us to hide His Word in our hearts so that we will not sin against Him. It is not always easy to obey God's Word, but the Holy Spirit gives us strength so we can do what God tells us to do. ♥

Every day Missy and Bill's mom and dad prayed about Dad's job. Missy and Bill didn't understand what was wrong, but they knew their mom and dad trusted God.

One day their dad did not go to work. After breakfast he read Matthew 6:24 to them. Then he said, "In this verse Jesus teaches us that we cannot serve two masters. A master is an owner. Everyone belongs either to God, or they belong to Satan. God loves us so much that He gave His Son Jesus to pay for our sins so that He could buy us back from Satan. Now we belong to God's family because Jesus paid for us with His own life. He is our Master, our Ruler, and our King. We are to serve Him with our whole hearts. Sometimes that is a hard thing to do, but we must always be loyal and obedient to our King."

Then their mom said, "Your dad had to make a very difficult decision. His boss at work wanted him to be dishonest about some things. Your dad would not do that because Jesus is His King. His heart is loyal to God. His job cannot be his master, so he had to quit his job."

"Missy and Bill," said their dad, "we don't want you to worry. We will trust God to give me another job. We must serve God in our work. If my job makes me disobey God, then I must quit that job. God is our Master, and He is also our heavenly Father. He will take care of us."

"But where will we get money to buy food?" asked Missy.

"I've got some money in my bank," said Bill. "Dad, you can have my money."

"My birthday is next week," said Missy. "You can have the birthday money Grandpa and Grandma send me."

"I may not have a job," said their dad, "but I'm a rich man. I have children who have a servant spirit rather than a selfish spirit. Missy and Bill, I'm very thankful for God's grace in you. We know it's God's will for me to provide for our family. I'm sure that the Lord will take care of us."

LET'S TALK

What is a master?

Who is our Master, Ruler, and King?

Is Jesus the Master of our work?
Is He the Master of our money?
Is He the Master of our time?

There are six words in Matthew 6:24.
Say this verse six times.

Say the verses for G through I.

LET'S PRAY

Thank God that He is your Master.
Ask Him to give you grace to serve Him
in everything you do.

Oh, give thanks to the Lord, for He is good!

PSALM 118:1

· ♥ ·

God is good, and it is impossible for Him to do anything that is not good. God is also sovereign. That means He is in control of everything that happens. ♥

Every day Missy and Bill's family prayed that the Lord would provide a job for Dad. One night before dinner, their dad read Psalm 118:1.

After they thanked God for their food, their dad said, "What does God tell us in Psalm 118:1 that we are to do?"

"We're to give thanks," said Bill. "Does that mean that we should give thanks that you don't have a job?"

"Well, Bill, we're to thank God because He is good. He's also sovereign. God is in control of when I will get a job, and since He's good, He will provide a job at just the right time. Whatever He gives us, or whatever He doesn't give us, it's because He is good, and He knows what's good for us. So we should always thank Him."

A few days later Missy and her mom were at the mall. Missy saw a doll in a store window. She thought it was the most beautiful doll she had ever seen. "Oh, Mom," she said, "may I please get that doll?"

"Missy, remember your dad doesn't have a job. We must

be very careful not to spend any extra money. We can't buy a doll."

Missy started to pout. She felt mad and sad. Then she remembered some of the verses hidden in her heart. She thought about how we cannot serve two masters. She knew that if she was selfish and angry, she would be serving Satan. But she really wanted the doll, and it was hard not to be resentful. Then she remembered the verse *"I can do all things through Christ who strengthens me."* In her heart she said, *"Dear Jesus, help me to serve You and not to serve Satan."* Then she remembered Psalm 118:1. She smiled at her mom and said, "That's all right, Mom. I'll give thanks to the Lord anyway."

"Missy," said her mom, "you just won a spiritual battle. Our enemy Satan wanted you to pout and complain, but the Holy Spirit gave you the victory. God's Word is like a weapon that we can use to fight Satan. I give thanks to the Lord because He's good, and I see His goodness in you."

LET'S TALK
Why do we give thanks to the Lord?

Is God good, even when we don't get things we want?

Say Psalm 118:1 three times.

Say the verses for J through L.

LET'S PRAY
Thank the Lord that He is good and that He always does what is good.

Praise the Lord! For it is good to sing praises to our God.

PSALM 147:1

■ ♥ ■

To praise the Lord means to adore Him, to thank Him, to worship Him, to exalt Him, to recognize that He is our King. ♥

Missy and Bill's dad read Psalm 147:1. As they ate yummy homemade pizza, their mom and dad asked them questions.

"Does Psalm 147:1 say that we are to praise the Lord when everybody is nice to us and when we get everything we want?" asked their mom.

"No," said Bill thoughtfully. "It just says, 'Praise the Lord.'"

"That's right, Bill," said his mom. "We're to praise the Lord all the time."

"Now *why* do you think we should praise the Lord?" asked their dad.

"Because He's our King," said Missy.

"And He loves us and takes care of us," said Bill.

"And because He gave Jesus to die for our sins," added Missy.

"You're exactly right," said their dad. "We should praise the Lord because of who He is and what He does."

"I have another question," said their mom. "Why is it *good* for us to sing praises to our God?"

This question baffled Missy and Bill. They knew that it was

good to praise the Lord, but they could not explain why.

"I'll help you." Their mom smiled. "First, it's good to praise the Lord because it pleases Him. Second, when we praise the Lord, it makes us think about Him rather than about our troubles. We praise Him because He is our sovereign King who is in control of everything. We praise Him because He is our heavenly Father who loves us and takes care of us. And when we praise Him, we stop worrying about what's happening to us. We start rejoicing that we have such a wonderful God."

"I think I understand," said Missy. "We praise God instead of worrying. When we praise God, we remember that He'll take care of us. We're not worrying about Dad getting a job."

"Oh, Missy, you do understand," said her mom.

"There's something else I want you to notice about this verse," said their dad. "It says that it's good to *sing* praises to our God. We can sing praises to God with our voices, or we can sing in our hearts."

"Now I have a wonderful surprise for you," said their mom. "God has provided a job for Dad. Let's praise the Lord."

LET'S TALK
Why should we praise the Lord?
Why is it *good* to praise the Lord?
Say Psalm 147:1 three times.
Say the verses for M through P.

LET'S PRAY
Praise the Lord for who He is and
for what He has done for you.

Quench not the Spirit.

1 THESSALONIANS 5:19 KJV

■ ♥ ■

To quench means to put out. The spirit is God's Holy Spirit who lives in our heart. ♥

One night Missy and Bill's dad read 1 Thessalonians 5:19. "What does that mean?" asked Bill.

"Do you remember when we were burning leaves and the fire got too big," asked his dad. "What did we do?"

"You got the hose and put water on it," said Missy.

"That's right. We quenched the fire. We put the fire out by pouring water on it. First Thessalonians 5:19 tells us *not* to quench the Spirit. When we sin, we quench the Holy Spirit. When we sin, we do to the Holy Spirit what water does to a fire."

"Let me give you an example," said their mom. "Last Sunday I helped in the nursery during Sunday school. The person who was supposed to help during church didn't come, so I had to stay. I thought about Philippians 2:14, 'Do all things without complaining and disputing.' I acted nice on the outside, but inside I grumbled and complained. I thought about how unfair it was that I had to stay in the nursery and take someone else's turn. The Holy Spirit reminded me of God's Word, but I quenched the Spirit's work in my heart because I did not obey the Word."

"I have an example," said Missy. "This afternoon when you

told me to pick up my toys and get ready for dinner, I complained. I thought about the verse, 'Children, obey your parents in all things, for this is well pleasing unto the Lord.' But I didn't want to stop playing. I guess I quenched the Spirit because I didn't obey the verse when I thought about it."

"Good example, Missy," said her dad. "When the Holy Spirit reminds us of God's Word, and we disobey, it's like throwing water on a fire. Sin quenches the work of the Holy Spirit in our hearts. But there's more! The Holy Spirit doesn't just remind us of God's Word. He also gives us power to obey it. When He reminds us, and we don't want to obey, we can ask Him to give us power to want to do what He tells us to do."

"That's what happened to me in the nursery," said Mom. "I asked the Lord to forgive me for complaining and disputing. I asked Him to give me grace. I started thinking about how much Jesus loves the little children, and I became thankful for the privilege of taking care of His little ones. God's Spirit is so powerful that He can change us. He doesn't just tell us what we are to do; He gives us power to do it."

I E T ' S   T A L K

What quenches the Holy Spirit?

What can we do when we don't want to obey God's Word?

Say 1 Thessalonians 5:19 three times.

Say the verses for A through E.

L E T ' S   P R A Y

Ask the Lord to give you power to remember His Word and to obey it.

Remember the Sabbath day, to keep it holy.

EXODUS 20:8

■ ♥ ■

The word Sabbath *means rest.* Holy *means set apart.* ♥

"Mom, Dad," called Missy and Bill, "Matt invited us to go camping with his family tonight."

"Sit down, kids, and let's talk about this," their dad said. "It's nice of Matt to invite you, but today is Saturday. What is tomorrow?"

"Sunday," said Missy.

Their dad opened the Bible and read Exodus 20:8. Then he said, "The Sabbath is the day God set apart for us to rest from our work, to think about Him, and to worship Him. Of course, we should think about Him and worship Him every day, but the Sabbath is a special day. One way we keep it holy is by gathering with other Christians to worship our heavenly Father together. Let me tell you why we rest from our work and worship God on Sunday. Look at this calendar. What is the first day of the week?"

Missy and Bill answered together, "Sunday."

Their dad said, "When Jesus died on the cross for our sins, His disciples laid His body in a tomb. Three days later something wonderful happened. Listen as I read from God's Word and see if you can tell me what day this amazing thing happened."

. . . as the first day of the week began to dawn, Mary Magdalene and the other Mary came to see the tomb. And behold, there was a great earthquake; for an angel of the Lord descended from heaven, and came and rolled back the stone from the door and sat on it. . . . The angel . . . said to the women, "Do not be afraid, for I know that you seek Jesus who was crucified. He is not here; for He is risen, as He said." (Matthew 28:1-6)

"Which day of the week did Jesus come back alive?" asked Dad.

"The first day," Missy and Bill answered.

"That's right," said their mom. "Sunday is our Sabbath, because that's the day Jesus rose from the dead."

"Missy and Bill," said their dad, "camping is fun, but there is nothing as exciting as gathering with God's people to celebrate that we have a risen Savior. God commands us to keep the Sabbath holy, and I don't want you to miss the blessing God has for you when you honor His day."

L E T ' S   T A L K

What does Sabbath mean?

What happened on the first day of the week?

Which day is the first day of the week?

Say Exodus 20:8 three times.

Say the verses for F through J.

L E T ' S   P R A Y

Thank God that Jesus rose from the dead so we can have rest in our souls. Thank Him for your church.

Seek the Lord while He may be found.

ISAIAH 55:6

■ ♥ ■

We must seek the Lord in His Word. Jesus is the treasure we find in God's Word. ♥

"It's a treasure hunt day!" said Missy and Bill's mom one Friday afternoon.

"Yea!" yelled Missy and Bill. They quickly started looking for their treasures. On treasure hunt days their mom hides something that Missy and Bill have to find. The treasure gives them a clue about a special treat they will have when Dad comes home from work.

Missy and Bill looked in all the closets, under the beds, under the pillows, behind the couch, and even in the refrigerator.

"We can't find it anywhere," wailed Missy playfully.

"Keep looking," said her mom. "Sometimes you have to seek long and hard to find a hidden treasure. Sometimes you miss it the first time you look, and you need to look a second time."

"Let's look under the beds again," suggested Bill. When they looked under Bill's bed, Missy noticed a pair of her dad's shoes.

"Is that it?" she exclaimed as Bill pulled the shoes out.

"Here's the clue. It's inside Dad's shoes."

They laughed as they each held up a flashlight.

"Why do we have flashlights?" Missy and Bill asked.

"Let's think about this clue," said Mom. "When do you need a flashlight?"

"When it's dark," Missy replied.

"We don't need a flashlight in the house because we can turn on a light," said their mom. "But if we're outside at night, we need a flashlight. You'll need a flashlight tonight because we're going camping!"

"This is a great treasure," said Missy.

That night, as they sat around the campfire roasting marshmallows, their dad read Isaiah 55:6 to them. "You know how you had to seek for the treasure this afternoon?" he asked. Missy and Bill nodded. "We must seek for the Lord. We must look for Him in His Word. When we read, study, and memorize God's Word, we understand more and more about Him. There are lots of treasures in the Bible. The treasure is God's truth. The treasure is Jesus, because He's the truth. Your mom and I pray that you will always seek the Lord."

LET'S TALK
Where do we seek for the Lord?
Say Isaiah 55:6 three times.
Say the verses for K through O.
LET'S PRAY
Ask God to help you find the treasures
He has for you in His Word.
Ask Him to help you know Him better.

Thou shalt not steal.

EXODUS 20:15 KJV

■ ♥ ■

God tells us not to take things that do not belong to us. God gives us grace to obey His commands. ♥

Miss Carolyn is a special friend to the children in Missy and Bill's neighborhood. They all love Miss Carolyn, and know that she loves them. She has a beautiful flower garden with roses, daffodils, tulips, begonias, peonies, and many more colorful flowers throughout the year. The children know how much she loves her garden and how hard she works in it. They are careful not to let their balls go into the garden.

One day Missy stopped to look at Miss Carolyn's garden. As she admired all the flowers, she noticed some she had never seen. They were different colors, and they looked as if they had little faces. *Mother would love these*, thought Missy as she picked a bouquet.

As she ran into her house, Missy called, "Mom, look what I brought you!"

"Missy," said her mom, "these pansies are beautiful. Where did you get them?"

Missy's big smile disappeared. "Mom," she gasped, "I took them from Miss Carolyn's garden without asking. That's stealing! What should I do?"

"You must tell Miss Carolyn what you did, and you must tell her that you're sorry. I'll go with you, Missy. I know you didn't steal on purpose. You just didn't stop and think. This will help you learn always to be careful and to think before you act. Let's pray and ask God to help you think of something you can do to pay Miss Carolyn for taking her flowers."

After they prayed, Missy and her mom walked to Miss Carolyn's. Missy told her what she had done. "I'm sorry. Please forgive me," said Missy as tears rolled down her cheeks.

Miss Carolyn hugged Missy and said, "God always forgives me when I do wrong. Of course I forgive you."

"Miss Carolyn, may I help you in your garden for a week to pay you back for taking the flowers?" asked Missy.

Miss Carolyn and Missy's mom thought that was a wonderful idea. Every afternoon Missy helped Miss Carolyn pull weeds and water the flowers. At the end of the week, as Missy and Miss Carolyn sat on the porch eating cookies and drinking lemonade, Miss Carolyn said, "Missy, I have a little gift for you. Here are some pansies for your very own to plant in your yard."

LET'S TALK

What did Missy do when she realized she had stolen Miss Carolyn's flowers?

How did Missy pay Miss Carolyn back for taking her flowers?

Say Exodus 20:15 three times.

Say the verses for P through S.

LET'S PRAY

Ask God to help you be very careful never to take anything that does not belong to you. Ask Him to help you to think before you act.

Unto Thee, O God, do we give thanks.

PSALM 75:1 KJV

■ ♥ ■

Psalm 75:1 teaches us that we should give thanks to God. We can have thankful hearts because God has saved us from our sin and has given us His Holy Spirit to live in us. ♥

One of Missy and Bill's favorite games to play when they are riding in the car is the "I'm thankful" game. They love it when one person describes something he or she is thankful for, and the others have to guess what it is.

"I'm thankful for something God has given me that lets me see my family and the trees and the clouds," said Missy.

"Your eyes," said Bill.

"Now guess what I'm thankful for," said Bill. "I'm thankful for something that teaches me what God wants me to know and what He wants me to do."

"The Bible," said Missy and her mom.

"It's your turn, Mom," said Missy.

"I'm thankful for the one who gives us the power to do what God tells us to do in His Word."

"The Holy Spirit," guessed Missy and Bill.

"Now it's my turn," said their dad. "I'm thankful for a day

of rest that God has set apart for His children to think about Him and worship Him."

"Sunday," said everyone at once.

"It's my turn again," said Missy. "I'm thankful for the place we go to on Sunday and the people we see."

"Our church," said everyone.

"We have time for one more," said Dad as he parked the car. "I'm thankful for two children who love the Lord Jesus and who ask Him for grace to let their light shine so that others see their good works and glorify their Father in heaven."

Missy and Bill had big smiles on their faces. "Us," they said.

LET'S TALK
Play the "I'm thankful" game.
Say Psalm 75:1 three times.
Say the verses for A through E.

LET'S PRAY
Thank the Lord that He is holy and good and loving.
Thank Him for something He has done for you.

Verily, verily, I say unto you, he that believeth on me hath everlasting life.

JOHN 6:47 KJV

■ ♥ ■

Not all Christians know the moment they were saved. The important thing is to know that we believe on Jesus, that we love Him, and that we want to obey Him. ♥

Before dinner Missy and Bill's dad read John 6:47. While they ate, they talked about the verse.

"Jesus said these words," explained their dad. "*Verily, verily* means truly, truly. Listen as I read John 6:47 again. Tell me what Jesus says we will have if we believe on Him. 'Verily, verily, I say unto you, he that believeth on me hath everlasting life.'"

"Everlasting life," answered Missy and Bill.

"That's right," said their dad. "This verse is a wonderful promise, and Jesus always keeps all of His promises. What is everlasting life?"

"I think it means that we'll live with Jesus in heaven," said Bill.

"That's right," Dad replied. "How long will we live with Him? How long is everlasting?"

"Forever," said Missy.

"Right again," said their dad. "We can't fully understand how long forever is or how we will live forever. We don't know everything about heaven. But we do know that heaven is real and that Jesus is there. Now here's another question. When does everlasting life begin?"

"When we go to heaven?" guessed Bill.

"Missy and Bill," said their dad, "Jesus said that whoever believes *has* everlasting life. We don't have to wait until we go to heaven. When God gives us grace to believe that we are sinners and grace to ask Jesus to be our Savior, He gives us spiritual life, or everlasting life, right now. His Holy Spirit lives in us so that we can believe and obey God's Word."

Bill was very quiet as they finished dinner. Finally his mom asked, "Bill, are you all right?"

"I've been thinking," said Bill. "I'm a sinner. I want everlasting life. I want Jesus to be my Savior."

The angels in heaven rejoiced, and Bill's mom and dad rejoiced, and Missy rejoiced as Bill asked Jesus to be his Savior.

LET'S TALK
What does Jesus promise that we will have if we believe on Him?

Does Jesus always keep all of His promises?

Say John 6:47 three times.

Say the verses for F through I.

LET'S PRAY
Thank God that He gives us everlasting life when we believe in Jesus.

We love Him because He first loved us.

■ ♥ ■

We love Jesus because He loved us first. Because of our sin, we could not love Jesus first. Jesus loved us and died on the cross so that we can be free from sin. Jesus did not die for us because we loved Him. He died for us because He knew that we could not love Him unless He freed us from sin. We are able to love Him and love others because He first loved us. ♥

Missy and Annie were visiting Ginger. Ginger showed them her new chalkboard. "There's only room for two of us to draw," said Ginger. "Here, Annie," she said as she handed Annie a piece of chalk. "We'll draw first."

Ginger and Annie drew funny pictures on the board. They whispered to each other and then said, "Missy, these are of you. You sure are funny looking," they teased.

Missy's feelings were hurt. She tried not to cry. She wanted to go home. Then she remembered 1 John 4:19. *Jesus loved me when I didn't love Him*, she thought. *Because He loves me, I can love Ginger and Annie even when they are not showing love to me. Please, dear Lord*, she prayed silently in her heart, *give me grace to show Your love to Ginger and Annie.*

Missy smiled and said, "You draw good pictures. That looks just like me."

All three girls laughed. Then Ginger gave

Missy the chalk and said, "Here, Missy, you draw some pictures now."

"Missy," said Annie, "I'm sorry. We were mean to you. Why didn't you get mad at us?"

"Because I remembered that Jesus loves me, and I prayed that He would help me to love you," said Missy. "The Holy Spirit reminded me of some of the Bible verses that are hidden in my heart. I wanted to say something unkind, but I remembered that 'I can do all things through Christ who strengthens me.'"

"Wow," said Annie. "I wish I had some Bible verses hidden in my heart. Will you teach us some verses, Missy?"

"Sure," said Missy. "Let's play Sunday school. I'll write a letter on the chalkboard and then teach you a verse to go with the letter."

LET'S TALK

Did Jesus love us first, or did we love Jesus first?

How does it make you feel when you think about Jesus loving you even before you loved Him?

Say 1 John 4:19 three times.

Say the verses for J through M.

LET'S PRAY

Thank God that Jesus loved us first so that we can love Him. Ask Him to help you show His love to others.

EXcept ye be converted, and become as little children, ye shall not enter into the kingdom of heaven.

MATTHEW 18:3 KJV

— ▪ ♥ ▪ —

Convert *means to turn away from sin and turn to Jesus in faith.* ♥

Bill and Missy's dad read Matthew 18:3. "Before you hide this verse in your hearts, I want to tell you about it," he said. "One day the disciples asked Jesus, 'Who is the greatest in the kingdom of heaven?' As they waited for His answer, perhaps each one hoped that Jesus would say that he was the greatest. Jesus did something that shocked the disciples. He called a little child to come to Him. The child probably ran up to Jesus, and I can imagine Jesus swooping the child up in His big, strong arms. Then Jesus said to His disciples, 'Except ye be converted, and become as little children, ye shall not enter into the kingdom of heaven.' Now let me ask you a question. What did Jesus say we have to become like to enter the kingdom of heaven?"

"Little children," Missy said.

"Did Jesus mean that the disciples had to become little boys?" asked Bill in amazement.

"No, Bill," said his dad. "He said they had to become *like* little children. Do you remember last week when you climbed our tree?"

"Sure," replied Bill. "I climbed up so high I was afraid to come down."

"I begged him to come down, but he wouldn't," said Missy. "I was scared he would fall, so I ran and called you."

They all laughed as their dad continued, "When I got there, you were glued to that tree. But when I told you that I would catch you if you fell, you slowly reached your foot down to the next limb, and then you stretched the other foot to the next limb, until you were in my arms. Bill, why didn't you come down when Missy tried to get you to?"

"I knew *you* could catch me if I fell, but she couldn't," said Bill.

"Exactly," said his dad. "You trusted me. Jesus wants us to trust Him just as a little child trusts his daddy. We are to turn away from our sin and trust Jesus to save us. Then we enter the kingdom of heaven."

"I'm glad we're hiding this verse in our hearts," said Missy. "I like to think about Jesus with a little child on His lap."

LET'S TALK

What does *converted* mean?

When we turn away from sin and turn to Jesus, what kingdom do we enter?

Say Matthew 18:3 three times.

Say the verses for N through P.

LET'S PRAY

Thank God that He is your King and that you are part of His kingdom. Ask Him to give you grace to glorify Him in all you do.

You are My friends if you do whatever I command you.

JOHN 15:14

■ ♥ ■

God tells us His commands in the Bible. The Holy Spirit gives us power to love God and obey His commands. ♥

Missy had dreaded this day. It was the day Ginger's family would move far away. When the men closed the big doors on the moving van, Ginger and Missy hugged.

"I'll miss you," Ginger said.

"I'll miss you too," said Missy.

Missy and her mom watched Ginger's family drive away. They went inside, and Missy sat on her mom's lap. "Why do friends have to move away?" she cried.

"I know it hurts when friends move," said her mom. "You can write letters to Ginger, and you can call her on the telephone, but it's not the same as having her next door."

After a few minutes Missy's mom said, "I know you feel sad, but I want to tell you about a Friend who will never leave you. He's the best Friend you will ever have. Do you know whom I'm talking about?"

"Daddy?" asked Missy.

"Missy, you have a Friend who loves you even more than your dad. Jesus said, 'You are My friends if you do whatever I command you.' The God of heaven and earth says that we are His friends."

"Wow!" exclaimed Missy. "Jesus says we're His friends?"

"Let's think about some ways that Jesus is our best Friend," suggested her mom. "Sometimes friends move away, but Jesus will never leave us. Sometimes friends are unkind, but Jesus always loves us. Sometimes friends can't do the things they say they will do, but Jesus is able to keep every promise. He's our very best Friend because He gave His life so that we can live with Him forever."

Missy looked happier. Her mom said, "Listen to John 15:14 again. What are Jesus' friends to do? 'You are My friends if you do whatever I command you.'"

"We're to do what He commands," answered Missy.

"How do we know what He commands us to do?" asked her mom.

"He tells us in the Bible," said Missy.

"That's right," Mom replied.

Missy was quiet for a few minutes. Then she said, "I'm sad that Ginger moved away, but I sure am glad that I have a Friend like Jesus."

LET'S TALK
What does Jesus say His friends will do?
What has Jesus given so that we will know His commands?
Whom has Jesus given so we can obey His commands?
Say John 15:14 three times.
Say the verses for Q through U.

LET'S PRAY
Thank Jesus that He is your best Friend.
Ask Him to help you do what He commands you to do.

Zacchaeus, make haste and come down, for today I must stay at your house.

LUKE 19:5

■ ♥ ■

When Jesus saves us, we are never the same. He gives us a new heart that loves Him and wants to obey Him. ♥

"We are going to hear an exciting Bible story today," said Mr. Logan. The boys and girls in the Sunday school class loved to hear Mr. Logan tell Bible stories. He began:

"*Jesus entered Jericho to pass through the town. In the city there lived a man named Zacchaeus. . . .*"

"So who is the man in Jericho?" asked Mr. Logan.

Julie raised her hand and answered, "Zacchaeus."

"Listen and see if you can tell me something about him," said Mr. Logan.

"*Zacchaeus wanted to see Jesus, but he was short and there was a large crowd. So he ran ahead and climbed up into a sycamore tree to see Him, for He was coming that way.*"

Missy raised her hand and said, "He wanted to see Jesus, but he was too short, so he climbed up in a sycamore tree."

Mr. Logan smiled and continued the story:

"*Zacchaeus sat in the tree and waited. He heard the happy voices of the crowd. He saw their smiling faces. Best of all, he saw Jesus. Of course,*

no one noticed Zacchaeus perched in the tree until an incredible thing happened.

"Jesus stopped. He looked up in the tree and said, 'Zacchaeus, hurry and come down, for today I must stay at your house.'

"Zacchaeus could not believe what he heard. Jesus wanted to go to his house! Zacchaeus scrambled down the tree and ran to his house as fast as his short little legs would carry him. When he got there, he welcomed Jesus into his home.

"The people were shocked that Jesus went to Zacchaeus' home because Zacchaeus was not a nice man. He cheated people and took their money. But Zacchaeus looked at Jesus and said, 'Lord, I will give half of my goods to the poor; and if I have cheated anyone I will pay them back four times more than I took from them.' Zacchaeus realized that Jesus was his Friend, and he wanted to do what Jesus commanded. Then Jesus said, 'Today salvation has come to this house.'"

Then Mr. Logan looked intently at the boys and girls. "Jesus went to Zacchaeus' house, and Zacchaeus was never the same. Jesus changed Zacchaeus' heart. When Jesus lives in our hearts, He changes us. He gives us the power to know Him and to obey Him. He is a wonderful Savior."

LET'S TALK
Why did Zacchaeus want to give money to the poor?

Say Luke 19:5 three times.

Say the verses for V through Z.

LET'S PRAY
Thank God that when Jesus lives in our hearts, He changes our hearts so that we want to obey Him.

K H D

V O

E U

C

J

M Q

S

T

L

P

A B

G

W

N R